LOST DOG

A True Story of Faith

BY JENNIFER FREY

Published by: BLUE MOUNTAIN MEDIA
              Publishing Division

Corporate address:
              11520 Jefferson Blvd., Suite 224,
              Culver City, CA 90230

Contact: jfreylac@gmail.com

Library of Congress Cataloging-in-publication
LOST DOG – A True Story of Faith/Jennifer Frey
ISBN-13: 978-1496194602
ISBN-10: 1496194608

Printed in the United States of America
Available through Amazon.com

ACKNOWLEDGMENTS

My thanks and gratitude to my dear husband, John, who has shown me what real love is by supporting me, helping me, guiding me and caring for me through the peaks and valleys of this amazing journey.

Also, many thanks to the friends and family whose loving support and prayers played an integral part in this story.

I now thank God every day for blessings too abundant to list.

<u>FORWARD</u>

Quiet your mind. What are you thinking about?
The quality of our thoughts can create health,
peace, and joy in our life - or create fear, suffering,
dis-ease, and injury.

For over twenty years, and working with over a
thousand patients in my private counseling
practice, I've observed how our thoughts direct our
emotions, how our emotions direct our actions,
and how our actions direct our life experience. The
question is, who directs our thoughts?

Lost Dog is a story about the search for a missing
dog --- It is a book about a first-hand experience of
letting go of who we think we are and trusting in a
relationship with a higher power to direct our
thoughts. It is a book about a woman's relationship
with her horse, her dog, significant loss, her
partner, her mind, her body, people in her life,
nature, activity and non-activity. But most

importantly, it's about her relationship with her God. It is about faith, trust and gratitude.

My patients have consistently taught me that an active and grateful relationship with a deeper power is the ultimate path to health, joy, and peace. Wherever you are in that journey – whatever your thoughts and a belief in a God or higher power - this book takes you through real life events that will stir your soul, and your emotions.

There are many name designations used to describe the "other" this nonmaterial relationship – God, Great Spirit, Jesus Christ, higher power, Lord, Yahweh, to name a few. Whatever your designation may be, I have learned, both personally and professionally, that the initiation of our inner listening and interaction within this transcendent affiliation is the most powerful and healing experience of all.

This book will inspire you.

It will invite you to a knowing you hold deep inside.

Patricia Starr, M.A., LMHC

<u>CONTENTS</u>

BEFORE THE STORY
<u>TRUE FAITH</u>

According to Wikipedia, faith is confidence or trust in a person, thing, deity, in the doctrines or teachings of a religion, or view without empirical evidence. The word faith is often used as a conceptual synonym for hope, trust, belief or knowledge.

We are well aware that faith is only justified if there is evidence to back it up. Evidence-based faith is the normal concept on which we base our everyday lives.

Faith in God according to the Christian perspective is based on the work and teachings of Jesus Christ. It sees the mystery of God and his grace and seeks to know and understand an active life aligned with the ideals portrayed by his example. To a Christian, faith is not static but causes one to learn more of

God and grow. It causes change as it seeks a greater understanding of God.

****

I purchased True Faith in June of 2006.

As a child and young adult I rode and trained horses for many years. It had been almost three decades since I had owned my own horse when life circumstances finally allowed for the opportunity again. The young, handsome, athletic and smart horse that I picked out was an off the racetrack thoroughbred. His Jockey Club registered name was True Faith. I called him "TJ".

My thinking when I first brought TJ home was that with all my experience with horses I would get him trained to submit to my every request in no time. What happened over the next several years was very different than what I had envisioned. Little did I know how much he would challenge me and that he would play a role in one of the most profound shifts of my life. What I thought would be a piece of cake - in the end required me to truly understand true faith.

Some people have an inner wiring to be successful. Our culture generally measures success by what we have and what we have accomplished in our lives. By all appearances I am "successful". Over the years I have accomplished a lot. With my wonderful, loving, caring husband we live in a beautiful place. I have good relationships with friends and family and co-workers. My career in the holistic healthcare field allows me to be my own boss and make a good living in a relaxed environment. And, I get to help people. My hobby with horses has given me many hours of pleasure and excitement in my free time. I should be happy, right?

I wish we had a template for life - because somewhere along the way something went wrong. After nearly ten years of "success" I was running on empty. Even though I had all the boxes ticked, I was not happy. My care and compassion for others was immensely depleted and I had lost my compass as to what was important in life. With a family history of depression and dysfunction I fell into a pattern of bad habits.

It finally hit me - I knew I needed to make dramatic changes in my life – not the outside but, the inside.

A thorough self-evaluation lead me to conclusion number one. I called myself a Christian but was not walking the path. Growing up in a Christian family, as a child I went to church and Sunday school, studied the bible, and had instilled good values and principles. I knew what a difference God can make in our lives, yet as an adult I was not following this path. I am writing my story because I was lucky enough to be hit on the head with a 2x4 and still have my life intact. The lessons learned are so profound I have to share them.

That template I said I wish we had - we have it - it is called the Bible, God's word, the Truth. My first step in rehabilitating my bad attitude, in finding what was missing inside of me, in correcting my bad habits was just to start reading. I had never read the whole Bible and as an adult never more than a chapter or verse here and there. It was time. Lucky for me my mom handed me "The One Year Bible" which lays out daily readings in easy digestible bits. I was off and running.

Over the next two years I made a commitment to the Christian faith and principles. I made a conscious decision to develop a closer relationship with Jesus and to understand what that meant for my life – something I had never *really* done as an adult.

In today's world there are thousands of resources on any topic – all you have to do is look. I came across a number of very inspiring and helpful books, in particular are two daily devotionals, one called "God Calling" and another called "Jesus Calling". These books just struck me of the power of having Jesus in your life. They offered the reminder that **if you are *really open and really listen* you will hear God talking to you.**

I was fortunate to have my own "wow" experience. From a spiritual perspective I was doing the work - praying, reading, studying, devotion, praying, reading, studying, devotion – waiting for the magic to happen. I had never had God talk to me before so I didn't know how this thing worked – but, one evening while I was praying and meditating, a date of January 14 kept popping into my head. As I was questioning this my answer came. "Yes, this is God ...*something* is going to change on January 14". I still wasn't sure what this meant and if it really was

God's voice. What was *something* and why January 14th? I wrote the date down in my journal and started waiting.

January 14...I was hit over the head...literally. My life was to change forever. The day started out as any normal Saturday – doing chores, cleaning house, nothing too earth shattering. By afternoon I had some free time and like I had done thousands of times before I went out to work with my horse, TJ, to spend time with him and do some training with him in the arena.

Then it happened, in a flash of a wink, I was standing beside him praising him, petting him for something he had just done well. I felt a blow to the front of my head as if someone had taken a 2x4 to it. My dear thousand pound horse had tossed his head up and with full force landed his jawbones square down on the top of my head at my front hairline. Ouch!...I was stunned; but, I did not pass out and I was not bleeding.

The condition of concussion was slightly familiar to me as my husband, John, had fallen off a horse and landed on his head a few years earlier; and, as a healthcare practitioner I had dealt with it in my practice on a number of occasions. John's situation was quite a scare as he lost a portion of his memory for about an hour and was a bit out of sorts for a couple days. However, he quickly returned to normal – no long term effects.

As I stood in the cold arena with TJ looking at me wondering what was wrong, I went through the checklist of the worrisome head injury symptoms – vision – ok, dizziness – no, memory – ok, I think, nausea – none, headache – not too bad. My self-diagnosis was that I was going to be okay. I felt a bit "funny" but I was sure that it would pass - if not in a few hours, surely within a few days. Little did I know that my life would not return to what I knew as "normal".

That January 14th afternoon I received a serious concussion, also called a traumatic brain injury. Since then I have had to adjust everything in my life. One article on this condition calls it "living with a borrowed brain". Once you have experienced it or know someone that has you will understand why.

Imagine waking up one morning to find that the most simple of tasks seem overwhelming -- making a meal, walking the dog and driving a car are suddenly major obstacles.

Most concussions heal within a month of the injury, but mine didn't. A small percentage of head injuries can take up to a year or longer – with new research now showing some can cause lasting or permanent cognitive changes. For more than two years and up to the present time I have been trying to recover a sense of "normal". As the doctors and specialists all say, the only real treatment is rest and time.

For much of the first year my mind was extremely foggy, each thought was like working through quicksand. The sensory system was on constant overload where sounds hurt and the bright light was piercing like fingernails on a chalkboard. Because my injury was to the frontal lobe anything emotionally out of the ordinary caused my brain to short circuit.

After a first week of hiding out in a dark room not able to move off the couch, somehow I managed to go back to work. By making dramatic adjustments to the scheduling and intensity of my day I was able to treat patients three days per week. Interestingly, the actual one-on-one work with patients was so instinctive and intuitive it wasn't as taxing to the injured part of my brain. The difficult part was that I could no longer multi-task and learning or tackling anything new was very challenging. Over time I have gotten to the point I can handle one simple job at a time.

The other important thing was if I was going to work it was vitally important that my "down" time was restful. Somehow I struck a balance between working for three days and doing next to nothing at home for the other four days of the week. My thanks to my dear husband who graciously picked up the slack at home and held me together when my senses were overloaded and I was falling apart.

The thing with a head trauma is, when the prescription is to rest and do nothing, it really means do nothing!! Have you ever tried to just do nothing? With most illnesses and conditions where you are laid up and ordered to rest you have the option of watching television, reading a book, going on the internet, catching up on phone calls or texting to friends. With a brain injury not only is it better not to so that the brain can rest - but, also most days your head is so exhausted and overloaded that you can't even bear the thought of asking the brain to do one more thing.

As each day passed and the progress was slow as molasses something inside my spirit and being needed to shift. What do you focus on for hours and days on end when you have to check out from the normal hustle bustle of life and you feel like you will never be normal again?

Funny how God works in our life to get his point across. As I stated earlier, prior to my injury I had already begun rejuvenating my spiritual path. Scriptures tell us over and over to step back out of the drivers' seat and let God lead our life. Because God granted us free will when He designed us it is one of the most difficult challenges we face on the Christian path. This was to be my lesson.

On most days it was extremely difficult to get my brain to do what I wanted when I wanted. I had to surrender. The only thing I could do was open myself up in prayer and ask God to fill my being and direct my course. The powerful thing is that when the brain and physical activity are taken out of the equation the only thing left is our heart and soul.

What I have realized, both through my work with people in a healing profession over the years and through my experience with a brain injury, is that life is delicate and complex. At the core of it all is our spiritual life and a single moment can change you in ways you never imagined.

In our culture so much of our identity is wrapped up in our ability to perform and do. My brain injury forced me to ask the question -- who am I, if not for my capacity to succeed and **do**? We live in a society that values **doing**. My journey has been the hugest blessing as it taught me to find peace in just **being**. But, the real power and the richest gift of all is that I learned how to let go and turn my life over to God's will and God's plan for my life.

As my husband, who has lived through this with me, can attest to - I have come an incredibly long way. I would say I am now at about 85% recovered. There is a huge possibility that I may never find that remaining 15%. A lot of activities are feeling more normal; however, the person I was before the accident has slipped away, and I am still trying to figure out what my life will be with my new identity.

Though I would not say it has been an easy journey, I feel tremendous gratitude for the lessons and insight gained through this experience. I feel a deep sense of peace and a joy that I cannot explain. The experience forced me to take myself out of the equation and turn my life and healing over to God's will. I am excited as I anticipate what my future will be. I now understand **TRUE FAITH**...

"True Faith" – TJ

Once upon a time……………

I lived in the rural Pacific Northwest.

We had a dog named Sadie…

<u>SADIE</u>

I grew up on a dairy farm in the beautiful rural
Pacific Northwest – an area with views of stunning
snow caped mountains at every turn and
thousands of acres of evergreen forest in your
backyard.   I have always loved the peacefulness
and serenity that living in this environment
surrounded by nature inspires. While in the hustle
bustle of a busy hectic life in Los Angeles, I met my
husband, John. It wasn't long before we both
agreed we wanted to escape that lifestyle and
move up to Washington State.

We did our research and ended up on the Olympic
Peninsula. Bordered by the Pacific Ocean on one
side and the Strait of Juan de Fuca on another, the
area is anchored by the majestic Olympic
Mountains and National Park. Close by are the
stunning lakes, waterfalls, rivers, mountains,
beaches and rain forest. In my opinion no other

place in America matches its diversity and natural beauty. Plus, the weather is fairly mild and it was a good place to start a business.

Soon after we moved, an interesting turn of events introduced to us a family who are now our good friends. They happened to own a spectacular seventy acre equestrian property. Their farm is nestled at the foothill of the mountains within shot of a view of the strait and across to Vancouver Island. It has miles of trails and facilities that would fulfill any horse lovers dream.

With my lifelong love of horses and desire to get back to nature it was almost as if by magic, or miracle, that we were offered to purchase a home and six acres as a part of their beautiful farm. We jumped at the chance.

We settled in to our new life in this quiet serene environment, but something was missing. No life is complete on a farm without man's best friend. John and I have no children together of our own so we felt that adding the four legged variety would be a nice addition to our family.

I quickly and easily found two of the big thousand pound equine variety. But, they lived out in the barn and were a bit more difficult to cuddle with. We needed a dog. So we put the word out.

We decided not to go the purebred route. Our thought was to find a mixed breed or rescue that just felt right. After several months and several tries, our neighbor, who had been taking her dog to obedience school for the third time, mentioned that her instructor was thinking of finding a new home for a dog that just didn't seem to fit into their pack.

We agreed to meet "Sadie". Our first impression was that she was beautiful and she was a good size

– about 50 lbs. She was a bit timid, but we could also see that she was very kind and sweet. In addition, she had lived with a professional dog trainer for four years so she had impeccable manners and training.

We decided to give it a try – agreeing that if it did not work out she would go back. It didn't take long to fall in love with her and know she was a "keeper". She had that intangible special quality.

From the beginning Sadie added a lot to our lives. She is definitely one of the extraordinary ones – tuned in to your thoughts and emotions and eager to please. If you are an animal lover and dog person you know what I mean.

Sadie's personality fit us to a tee. The longer we had her the more comfortable she was and the more we saw her true personality. We appreciate that she can be quiet and sweet and introspective, but also expressive and active and athletic.

She was meticulously trained and knows how to do what she is asked, do tricks and mind her manners. Trouble is she also has an independent streak where she chooses to disregard her training. (I am sure it drove her previous family crazy) She will come hang out with you ...if she feels like it. Come when she is called...if she feels like it. We look at it as the endearing side of her personality, more like a cat if you will.

We don't know for sure what her breeding is – based on her looks and her personality - a best guess is a mix of lab and whippet. Whatever it is, even though most of her life she has been a pampered indoor dog, she loves the outdoors and is hard wired for hunting and running and chasing.

Our beautiful property is surrounded on all sides with forest and trees with lots of wild life and room to roam and hike. For a dog like Sadie - heaven. She absolutely loves her walks in the woods!!! It gives her a chance to smell and sniff and pounce on things. The other thing that she absolutely loves is to run full speed just to blow off energy – the fit athletic girl that she is. Her absolute bliss when she is in her element is obvious and a lesson for us humans to learn from.

What we loved about Sadie would also become part of the double edge sword. We had to learn her idiosyncrasies the hard way. For a dog that loved to explore and run as much as she did we wanted to allow her as much freedom as possible. After a short time of getting to know her and building trust and relationship we let her go off the lead. We trusted her incredible training that she would come back to us if she ventured off too far.

This is how we discovered that Sadie had an instinct hard wired in her DNA to chase deer. In our beautiful natural surroundings encountering families of deer is a regular occurrence. It didn't take long for us to learn trust and relationship and training meant nothing when instinct kicked in. The first chance she had unencumbered by a lead or fence - our dear sweet usually obedient Sadie was off and running.

We were lucky the first time. It happened early in the day and after a couple hours of frantic searching – she came back to us. We had gone in the house to take a break from searching when John looked out the window and there she was trotting across the field coming toward home.

In finding a balance of giving her freedom to run and roam and our fear of losing her there have been a number of near misses where she ventured off but eventually we got her back.

We were trying to learn from our experiences. We discussed getting her a GPS collar of some sort. At the very least we were smart enough to put a tag on her collar with a name and phone number. As a last resort I also was working with a training shock collar that I could give her a "zap" when she spotted a deer and tried to run. However, we still didn't completely trust her without a lead.

One of the scariest near misses we had was the day she managed to go off and after five hours on a wet and rainy day we still hadn't found her in the usual places and she hadn't decided to return home on her own.

I know a lot of people have dogs that go off on an adventure for several days and eventually come back home – no problem. The fear we had for our dear Sadie was that we live so close to nature that real predators are right in our backyard. There have been regular sightings of cougars, bears, bobcats and coyotes. In addition to natural predators, there was also the chance if she were to find humans they would think she is so cute and sweet they might decide just to keep her.

We were beginning to panic when my husband received a call that someone had found her – six miles away!! It was not just any six miles away that Sadie had covered in only five hours. It was up and down a steep ravine through a creek and through heavy forest with possible dangers lurking at any turn.

She had come out in a logging area where some teenagers were riding dirt bikes and happened to spot her. They took the time to look at her tag and call us and then lead her from the area back in the woods out to the main road so that we could meet them and pick her up. With happy tears we loaded her into the car eternally grateful that we got our girl back.

Over the years we learned from the near misses when she did manage to escape. We now had to either to keep a lead on her or keep a close eye to make sure there are no deer within her field of vision. Which meant only letting her run free in certain situations. For the most part this worked. On the close calls with God on our side and a little luck we would always find her and get her back.

It had been over a year since Sadie had escaped...

Sadie

THE STORY
DAY ONE

It was a Tuesday in mid-February and I had worked all day. It had been just a little over a year since my True Faith head injury. I was coping with most things fairly well as long as there weren't extreme emotional or mental challenges. I was joyful on my way home that it was still light outside and that I would be able to see to enjoy doing my barn chores when I arrived.

Almost every day I had been hooking Sadie up to a lead to take her to the barn because I couldn't see the deer in the dark and I didn't want it to be on my watch that she took off and we lost her. This would be a chance for her to play and run a bit this trip out and I would/could keep a watch out for deer – besides she had her training collar on and I could "zap" her if anything happened. The time was about 5:30pm – that is about 45 minutes before dark in February in the Pacific Northwest.

We were on our way back from the barn - 20 yards from the house when we both spotted it – her friend the deer. We all stood frozen for a minute and then...she was gone. The hard wired instinctual drive that John and I always dreaded would take her from us one day - kicked in. She had the training collar on so I fumbled as quickly as I could to get into my pocket to pull out the control. By the time I did I could no longer see her, but I hit panic, panic, panic. I kept waiting to see her trotting back – disappointed of course that she could not catch her fleet footed friend.

By this time John heard the ruckus and came out of the house. We called and called for her...no Sadie. With the 45 minutes we had left till dark we frantically jumped into action. Flashlights in hand we drove around to the back of our property.

Hunting and hiking through the woods we quickly searched all the likely places we could get to...no Sadie. I was beginning to get that sick feeling in the bottom of my gut. The knowing that it would be dark soon and we would have to give up searching and spend our first night in four years in a quiet house without our best friend.

We were in shock! My dear John did his best to console me and reassure me that it was not my fault. "Do not blame yourself" he said. At the same time he was struggling to hold back his emotion and concern. While Sadie loves the great outdoors and she lives for her walks in our beautiful natural surrounding - she had been a pampered house dog and had never spent a night outdoors. We were concerned to say the least. Plus, if she could go six miles in five hours – she could be anywhere in the county by morning.

As I was committed to my renewed spiritual path this was my first real test. It was my chance to trust God's plan and turn it over. I read my devotion for the day. The way God works the words seemed to speak directly to me for this very moment, our very situation. All I could do at this point was pray. I used the phrase I had committed to months earlier - **I trust you Jesus**.

I did my best to get some sleep. My poor injured brain was trying to process what had happened and not doing a very good job. I was numb and overwhelmed.

You are feeling weighed down by a plethora of problems, both big and small. They seem to require more and more of your attention, but you must not give into those demands. When the difficulties in your life feel as if they're closing in on you, break free by spending quality time with Me. You need to remember who I AM in all My Power and Glory. Then humbly bring Me your prayers and petitions. Your problems will pale when you view them in the Light of My Presence. You can learn to be joyful in Me, your Savior, even in the midst of adverse circumstances. Rely on Me, your Strength. I make your feet like the feet of a deer, enabling you to go on the heights.

February 19th
"Jesus Calling" – by Sarah Young

THE STORY
<u>DAY TWO</u>

I had to go to work Wednesday morning. I have
been so absolutely lucky to work in an environment
with loving caring people. Sadie had been to work
with me on many occasions so as I spread the word
that she was missing I could not have received
more love, more caring and more support.

My hands were tied as far as doing the practical
things because I had to work and my head was
already overwhelmed. My job for the day, if you
will, was to enlist the caring loving support of those
around me to pray for Sadie's safety and protection
and ultimately, God willing, for her safe return.

Not everyone believes in God or easily understands
a universal energy and a higher power. The thing
about the people I work with is that they are
amazingly spiritual and intuitively gifted. In

addition, a number of my close friends and associates are strong Christians and believe in the power of prayer.

The immediate response I got, had it not been from my good friends and associates who I know are "tuned in", could easily be construed as just hoping for the best. At least three people I trusted said "I feel she is going to be okay". In addition, my close friend Jenn came to me part way through the day specifically reporting what she was intuitively picking up.

"Sadie is okay. She is not very far from home. She is in a wooded area. I can sense her navigating her way through the crunchy branches like in a forest. She is a little disoriented and was surprised that her humans didn't come to get her before it was night", and the funniest part which is so like Sadie - Jenn said Sadie was also easily distracted by what was going on around her but was doing okay.

Still in shock I wanted to believe them. But, the fear, the unknown, the real dangers – the doubt just wanted to creep in. Funny in situations like this you just want to know, have the answer, and the sooner the better. It is a real test of faith. Over the prior year so many of my lessons had all pointed to the same thing though – **Let go and trust God.**

While I was busy at work - John was busy with all the practical things. Maybe it was law of attraction, maybe it was just being one step ahead; but, we had made up "lost dog" signs about a month earlier. Just in case this ever happened John wanted to be prepared. He posted probably a hundred signs, went to all the vets to take them posters, called the radio stations who would announce it every hour, told the newspapers who put it on their Facebook page. He called the animal control, humane society, friends of animals in hope that someone somewhere would spot our Sadie. And, of course, he started searching.

It was so hard to stay at work and concentrate so I managed to finish a bit early and get home before dark so I could satisfy my urge to just go out and search and search - thinking the more we were out there the more chance of finding her. That is our human way of thinking not God's way.

As soon as I got home I headed out for a quick walk to search. It was beginning to get dark and I was returning from my walk when my phone rang. It was my friend and client Robin who I hadn't talked to in probably three years. She does intuitive readings and animal communication on a more professional level; and, grasping at straws I had called her early in the day hoping for some help. After sending her some pictures and basic information - thank goodness for modern technology – she was calling back.

I know a lot of people question intuitive or psychic powers. I have worked in the field of energy medicine long enough to not only believe they exist but have felt it myself. I believe it is one of God's many gifts if we choose to use it. In my own personal journey I have had a struggle to listen to and trust the intuitive information I receive as God's guidance. I will come back to this point later in the story.

So, Robin called back. The key points she was able to obtain from her reading gave us hope. One, she picked up on Sadie's personality almost exactly. She nailed the fact that Sadie loved and cared about us as her family; but, at the same time was very independent and liked to do her own thing and at times could even be bloody-minded. Anyway, we figured if she was so right about that then the rest could be true too.

The most important thing she said was that she felt that Sadie would be found and would be okay. Also, she said Sadie would be found by a nice family with a teenager and that she was fairly close by, maybe within three miles – which, where we live might as well be the whole county as far as searching goes. Robin also said that somewhere in her travels she would come across a classic red barn - you know the kind with the kind of rounded roof and the white "X's" on all the doors. Definitely not a lot to go on and definitely not rocket science; but, it was a start and it was hope.

As Wednesday drew to a conclusion and we headed into our second evening without our girl we tried to remain hopeful that she had just gone out on an adventure and soon we would have our friend back home.

It is amazing to me how God uses trauma and difficulties to draw us closer to him and closer to each other. I had been committed to reading my bible and devotion books for several years now. But, it is interestingly different when there is an acute emotional event to highlight its meaning for our life. My passage for this day from "God Calling" by A.J. Russell:

Claim Your Rights

"In everything by prayer and supplication let your requests be made known to God." But do not beg. Rather come just as a business manager bringing to the owner the needs, checks to be signed, etc. and to know that to lay the matter before him means immediate supply.

I long to supply, but the asking – or the faith-assurance from you is necessary, because to you that contact with me is vital.

I went to bed Wednesday night laying the matter before God. – Of course, hoping and praying that it would be his will to bring our Sadie home.

Learn to live from your true Center in Me. I reside in the deepest depths of your being, in eternal union with your spirit. It is at this deep level that My Peace reigns continually. You will not find lasting peace in the world around you, in circumstances, or in human relationships. The external world is in flux — under the curse of death and decay. But there is a gold mine of Peace deep within you, waiting to be tapped. Take time to delve into the riches of My residing Presence. I want you to live increasingly from your real Center, where My Love has an eternal grip on you. I am Christ in you, the hope of Glory.

February 20th
"Jesus Calling" – by Sarah Young

THE STORY
<u>DAY THREE</u>

By Thursday the exhaustion was starting to set in for me. My post-concussive brain was so overwhelmed I cannot even put it into words. My emotions were numb and I had a constant headache. John was dealing with the situation in his own way – staying vigilant with hope and doing practical things to help out. Thursday was my day off from work, so we were able spend some time together helping and supporting each other whenever the idea that we may never see Sadie again came into our heads. Sometimes I was the strong one and sometimes it was John.

Armed with the likelihood that she could be close by we had to do what we physically and humanly could - comb the woods and search trails - calling her name hoping that she would hear us calling and pop out and come running. We spent most of the morning out searching.

One blessing in all of this was that the weather was cooperating. It was a beautiful clear day with blue sky and hardly a cloud. All I had to do was just look around me to feel the appreciation and gratitude for all God had blessed us with. However, we finished our hikes still with no sign of our Sadie.

What felt strange now was daily routine without her. She had always been spoiled with three walks during the day so when the time came when she would usually be bugging one of us that it was "time" the house felt extremely empty. So without her John and I went out on yet another walk together in the afternoon to look some more, using the time to draw even closer and support each other in what we were going through.

By the time we got back I was exhausted. However, with the adrenaline coursing through my body I could not sit still. For a distraction I decided to go out to the barn and spend some time with TJ and soak up some of that pure and unconditional love that our animals always seem to share when we are feeling vulnerable.

As a coincidence, while I was at the barn one of our good friends Karen, and her teenage daughter, who I had taught riding lessons to for several years, arrived at the barn. They know Sadie, are animal lovers themselves, and had just gotten a new dog of their own. I was anxious to share the story of the last few days to enlist additional support and prayers.

On a number of levels this was valuable. They lived only a mile away so they could keep an eye out for Sadie. But, additionally I knew Karen was in a Bible study group with a number of our other friends that also lived close by. I knew she would spread the word and they would keep a watch in the neighborhood and keep Sadie in their prayers.

Meanwhile John could not sit still. While I was at the barn he went out for a drive just to look... I returned from the barn to our empty quiet house and collapsed into a big comfy chair. Now I really did need to take a break. With a damaged brain one of the conditions, if you will, is that when you are done you are DONE. Over the previous year I had gotten good at figuring this out. I have learned to stop, turn my brain off and rest.

Over and over in the Bible and in our Christian devotions we are told to put our own self aside and to allow God to take the reins. Because of my head injury my brain doesn't always do what I want. This means sometimes I have to turn over the reins whether I want to or not. When you are forced to *really* do this it highlights how little we *actually* do it and how resistant we are to it in our busy lives. We generally always want to stay in charge.

As I sat, exhausted, in my living room chair - my life was changing forever. I was finally giving up control. It is hard to explain the sensation that came over me as I sat looking out the window. It was partly just resting and part prayer and meditation. The feeling I had was a deep sense of peace and of a presence standing near me. I made the decision that I would trust God's voice speaking through me. Not only would I trust it but I would follow through with action on my part. Something I had hesitated to do previously in my life.

An hour and a half whizzed by. The overwhelming message I kept receiving regarding what I thought was to help find Sadie was a certain place we should go look for her. This is it I thought to myself. God is helping me locate her. I had to tell John. I would catch him on his way back from his drive. The place was a logging road about 2 miles from us and he could stop on his way by. But... That was not what God had planned for me.

By the time I called John he was already almost to our driveway and it seemed silly to send him back out. This was *my* message *my* inner prompting so I would be the one to follow through. Tired as I still was I jumped in the car and drove to the spot. I hiked in on the trail and started searching.

I looked around me – huge fir trees towered over me and the forest undergrowth was so heavy I could hardly find the path. The vastness started to overwhelm me. My doubts started to creep in. Logically - intellectually I knew the chances of finding Sadie in this spot were about the same as a needle in a haystack.

We had already searched so much with no success, why would this be any different? So, I started praying - not just any ole' prayer – the life or death – this is really important kind of prayer. It went something like this – "I know you can move mountains Lord – if we have faith...I know you are all powerful Lord. I know it is possible that you could plop Sadie down right here in front of me. **I believe...I trust you Jesus, I trust you Jesus, I trust you Jesus.** You know how important Sadie is to us and we would really really like to have her come back home." At this same time I looked up and around searching for Sadie, but also taking in the absolute splendor of where we live. So I added into my prayer – "thank you Jesus for this beautiful place we live."

I had been gone about forty minutes and had just sat down to collect myself and my thoughts. I was deep in meditation when my phone rang. Startling me out of my contemplative mode - it was John. Our neighbor had just called him to report that she thought she saw Sadie just moments prior at the back of their property!!!! Ahhhhh...this was the first possible sighting - the first bit of hope. God answering prayers?? – maybe. I raced back.

So, just two properties over and probably less than half a mile from our house - The neighbor had just seen a dog that she was 99.9% sure was Sadie. She had returned home from work and was looking at the back of her property when she spotted a dog. She had seen the posters John had posted and from the picture was sure it was our Sadie.

In describing the situation the neighbor said when she called to the dog it ran, which is very unlike Sadie; but, not knowing her current state of mind after two nights out on her own also very possible. Sadie could be so close to home yet so far away. Upon further investigation a deer had been killed and the carcass partially eaten. Sadie could be nearby. With just a little bit of time to search some more before dark with the possibility she could be within earshot there was a ray of hope.

As darkness edged in, however, still nothing. Even though we didn't find her - we had renewed faith that Sadie was okay and she was nearby. In some ways this was also confusing. If Sadie was so close, didn't she know home was right around the corner and she could come in for a nice big dish of kibble and a warm safe bed? If we could only go inside her head and know what she was thinking. With this new information I put in a call to my friend Robin to give her the updated information.

I went to bed again praying praying praying that Sadie would be safe out there in the wild and that soon she would come back home.

Trust and thankfulness will get you safely through this day. Trust protects you from worrying and obsessing. Thankfulness keeps you from criticizing and complaining: those "sister sins" that so easily entangle you. Keeping your eyes on Me is the same as trusting Me. It is a free choice that you must make thousands of times daily. The more you trust Me the easier it becomes. Thought patterns of trust become etched into your brain. Relegate troubles to the periphery of your mind, so that I can become central in your thoughts. Thus you focus on Me, entrusting your concerns into My care.

February 21st
"Jesus Calling" – by Sarah Young

THE STORY
<u>DAY FOUR</u>

I had to go to work again. This was good and bad.
It gave me a distraction from worrying and
something different to focus on. John had the
more difficult job. He was at home in the empty
house not knowing where to turn.

My intuitive friends were doing their best to help
with what information they could add. But, they
were not getting as much information as they did
the first couple days. However, the one thing in
common they kept reiterating was - she is very
close to home. Both Jenn and Robin even said she
could be as close as one quarter to a half mile.

Jenn had never been to our farm so she was just
going by the images she was getting a sense of.
Very strongly she was getting an area southeast of
our house on the edge of the forest and near a

huge ravine – a very difficult area to get through and navigate. To help us put everything in perspective we decided to add to our intuitive information by referring to modern satellite technology. We went on Google maps to survey the area and possibilities.

We hadn't really focused to the southeast yet – so, I relayed this information to John so he could try searching a new area. He had already planned to go around to meet the neighbors at the back of our property nearest where Sadie was likely spotted by the deer carcass. This was at least something new to focus on. By mid-day he was getting tired and needed a break as did I. He was coming in for lunch.

John's biggest question for Jenn was - can you tell if Sadie is still okay? - Can you pick up anything more to help us? The reason I bring this up is to just raise another instance of how powerful intuition can be.

The funny thing was, in the period of time that John was on his way into town, Jenn was busy working with a client. During this time her mind was distracted from her work and kept zeroing in on one thing - she very strongly picked up a sense of Sadie and the colors black and red. That is just weird you might say – but when you are receiving intuitive information your job is not to edit it but just report it. She was anxious to come out and tell me what she had been picking up. About this time John had arrived. We all sat down to chat for a minute so Jenn could share some of the information she was getting, including the red and black. We just had to smile – John was wearing black pants and a red sweatshirt! Okay so that doesn't help us find Sadie - it was just interesting.

Later in the day Jenn agreed that it would be helpful to actually come out to our place to get her bearings on what she was feeling and to see if anything on a specific location would come to her.

She volunteered to do so, but the timing of such couldn't happen till about 5:00 pm.

She arrived at our house a short time before me. John was still out looking. This gave her time to survey the immediate area and see if anything gave her a strong sensation. By the time I arrived she had received somewhat confusing information, in that, she felt Sadie in almost every direction she turned. We took that as a positive sign that Sadie was nearby – we just didn't know which direction.

We then headed out to where John was around back – the location that she had pointed out earlier in the day on the Google map. John had met the neighbors there, very nice people with a dog themselves, and had gotten permission to go looking and searching on their property.
So, we all headed in, climbing up and over the heavy undergrowth in the forest, through the ups and downs of the terrain – about a half mile into

the forest and we came to the edge of a ravine which dropped straight down at least 100 yards.

We looked and called, looked and called – no Sadie. We paused for a bit – "She has been here." Jenn reported what she was feeling. She could definitely feel Sadie's presence very strongly. Unfortunately though, she had come and gone.

We moved on to another location to continue to give Jenn a feel for the area and what the surrounding terrain and layout was like. By this time it was beginning to get dark and the weather was starting to shift. As we explored the territory, now with flashlights in hand, it was getting colder and there was light rain with slushy snow coming down. A slight worry for us, but we thought an even bigger worry for Sadie.

We were heading back to the car when Jenn stopped in her tracks. "This is it …I feel her here."

Again having hope we headed down a path lodged narrowly between the ravine that drops down to the creek below and the road that we had already been on a hundred times in the last three days. It was partly forested, not as difficult to navigate as where we had been earlier.

What was interesting as we walked through this area, besides the fact that Jenn was constantly feeling Sadie's presence very near to us, was that, despite the cold and slushy weather, it felt quite warm and cozy tucked into the woods in this way. There were a number of places that I thought – if I were a dog out overnight, this would be a nice warm safe place to hang out for a while. But, no sign of our girl.

With mixed emotions we had to head back to the house to face yet another night without our best friend. We thanked Jenn for her time and efforts.

At least her information gave us hope and an idea of where to search in the morning.

In an empty house, we were facing now a fourth night - waiting, wondering, hoping for Sadie to come back to us safe and sound. John and I drew closer together – saying our prayers and encouraging each to stay positive. We had to believe she would be okay.

We had a plan to get up and go search in the area where we were with Jenn at first daylight. We hoped that if that was where Sadie was most recently maybe we would spot her in the morning before she was on the move again for the day. Anyway, since it was the weekend now I would have more time to help in the practical way by going out searching.

I went to bed; my whole body was buzzing and vibrating from the intensity of the last few days.

The best analogy is that it was like having the accelerator of your car stuck all the way down and no way to turn it off. This for several months had been one of the issues I was dealing with my injured head, but the intensity of our current situation had exacerbated this symptom way beyond anything I had dealt with so far.

The only thing that would give me any peace was prayer and repeating my mantra of the year **I trust you Jesus, I trust you Jesus, I trust you Jesus.** Like I had probably already hundreds of times over the last few days I laid my humble request before God. "Please Lord I know you are all powerful, I know you can move mountains – We would really really appreciate it if you would bring Sadie back to us". It was then while I was saying my prayer and trying to fall asleep I heard God's voice speaking to me. I wasn't sure at the time, but now every time I tell the story I just have to smile.

"Jennifer, you are going to get Sadie back. It is not going to be this weekend – it is going to be Monday. I know being human you will have doubt – you will have to go out and search tomorrow and the next day. That is okay, but don't worry – Sadie will be back on Monday."

Okay then...I could get back to normal, quit worrying, and believe that we would see our Sadie in a couple days. Yeah right!?!? No, I am human too and it is the hardest thing in the world to just sit and wait – even when you hear His voice telling you it's okay. Of course I would stick with the plan for the morning – I had to do my part to help find our girl. Though, I did manage to fall asleep with peace in my heart and faith that Sadie would, in fact, be home by Monday night.

You need Me every moment. Your awareness of your constant need for Me is your greatest strength. Your neediness, properly handled, is a link to My Presence. However, there are pitfalls that you must be on guard against: self-pity, self-preoccupation, giving up. Your inadequacy presents you with a continual choice – deep dependence on Me, or despair. The emptiness you feel within will either be filled with problems or with My Presence. Make Me central in your consciousness by praying continually: simple, short prayers flowing out of the present moment. Use My Name liberally, to remind you of My Presence. Keep on asking and receive, so that your gladness may be full and complete.

February 22nd
"Jesus Calling" – by Sarah Young

THE STORY
<u>DAY FIVE</u>

Even before the crack of dawn both John and I
were awake with hope and anticipation and a plan
for the morning. I was still exhausted, but the
adrenaline pumping through my body got me up
and going. I know God's voice said Monday but I
wanted this to be the day we found Sadie.

As soon as it was light enough out, we headed off
to the area where Jenn had directed us to the
previous night. We started our search yet again.
Since it was the weekend and I didn't have to think
about work I was focused and eager to contribute
to the searching. We were hopeful as we headed
out. We spent a couple hours and again came up
with nothing.

We had combed this area thoroughly and it was
only about 8:00 am. John had done so much

walking and hunting and searching the previous several days that after a couple hours he was emotionally and physically spent. He headed back to the house to have some breakfast and get some rest.

I was determined this would be the day. There was much more territory to search and I planned to stay out till I covered it all. Shortly after John went back to the house and I was out on my own an incredible thing happened.

This is the day and age of smartphones. About six weeks earlier I had purchased a flashy new IPhone. Most people know your use of an IPhone is not complete unless you have the proper array of apps. One of the apps I had loaded on my phone was one with bible verses, so that I could conveniently have an inspirational verse at my fingertips should I so choose. I had not used it much and, in reality, had almost forgotten I had it.

However, on this particular day this app had a mind of its own and did something it had never done before. As I was hiking through the forest I heard my phone ring an alarm signaling that I had a message. Yet, rather than it being a text message or voicemail **—it was my bible verse app giving me the following verse: "This is the day the Lord has made, we will rejoice and be glad in it" Psalms 118:24.**

Wow...I still am amazed when I recall this happening. To this day my bible verse app has never given me a verse unless I intentionally go in and ask for it. What a way to change the intention of my day.

I was reminded...It was a picturesque day, the sun was out, the birds were singing, it was peaceful and serene and God's beautiful creation was in vivid display everywhere I turned. I was exploring nature and the stunning landscape that had been right in my backyard for the last six years. Yes, I was looking for Sadie – but at each step I was giving praise and gratitude for God's amazing gift of this magical world we live in and all that I did have in my life.

I continued searching with this renewed peace and joy in my heart. Another couple hours went by and I hardly noticed. While I was out I had a call from Robin just checking in with a bit more information. A new sense she was getting was that Sadie was, yes close to our house - maybe like within a half mile – but, also that she was southwest and just across the main road near our driveway.

We had been, for majority of our searching, covering the area mostly north and east. It was time to go back to the house, share this information with John and regroup. Besides, we had friends coming to help join in the searching.

An interesting question in all this is parallel to the point many people make about God and Christianity in general. How do you know anything is "real" if you can't see it, touch it, taste it or smell it? That is the essence of faith. Sometimes you just have to rely on that inner peace and inner knowing. We had no proof, no security that Sadie was anywhere close, or even still alive for that matter. She could have been eaten by a cougar or bear on the first night – Yet we had faith and hope and love and a confidence that the intuitive information we were receiving was valid.

I met John and our friends back at the house. The plan was that they would go all the way around to the back of our property and stay pretty much to the road and just hope to be at the right place at the right time if Sadie were to appear out of the woods. My job was to delve in to the new area – the southwest that Robin had described.

By now this was an adventure for me. I kept playing over and over in my head the bible verse that had popped up out of nowhere on my phone earlier in the day – "This is the day the Lord has made, we will rejoice and be glad in it". I was full of gratitude for all I did have on this lovely day. At the same time I continued to pray asking for Sadie to safely come home to us. Again I heard God's voice - "Something important is going to happen around noon today". It was already about 10:30ish so I didn't have to long to go. What possibly could God have in store for me?

My mission was to search this new area. I was actually quite intrigued with what I was discovering. It was a territory that I had driven by or ridden by on the horses numerous times but, it was hidden behind the trees and the broken down fence. This was my chance to explore. I was a bit nervous because I was trespassing on peoples' property, but I figured they would understand if I told them the story about Sadie being missing.

By about 11:30 I was getting tired and I called to check in with John and let him know where I was and what I was up to. Then I sat down for a rest and meditation in the forest with nature all around me. I could see the tracks through the trees - I'm sure worn by the numerous trips of the families of deer that live in the area.

Sitting still for a minute I realized how exhausted I was. But, after a rest I would persevere. I checked in with God with a prayer – not forgetting, of course, that earlier in the day I thought I heard Him say "something" would happen around noon. I repeated over and over "I trust you Jesus. I trust you Jesus. I trust you Jesus." I sat for a bit longer and meditated on God's power and will coming into my being – feeling the strength and peace that comes from allowing Him to lead our life.

Soon I got up and was ready to venture on. I headed west where I saw what looked like a clearing. The clearing opened onto a dirt road/ driveway. I absolutely could not believe my eyes!! There in front of me was the classic little red barn - complete with the white "X's" across the doors – the exact image that my friend Robin had described from her intuitive reading back on Wednesday night. Oh yes, and it was 12 o'clock. I could not wipe the smile off my face. While it wasn't Sadie – It was confirmation and it was hope.

I looked around. As I headed up to the house to knock on the door I noticed a little sign that said something to the effect that anyone who loves animals is welcome. Perfect – I thought. However, I knocked and waited a bit. Nobody home.

Alright I would just continue on - anything now was just icing on the cake. I followed the road in a ways further where I came upon another lovely farm nestled hiding way back in the woods. This next part of the story is now just a really interesting aside and not really related to searching for Sadie. But, I have added it in because it is still part of this amazingly profound week.

I was feeling pretty confident now and I thought I would go ahead and knock on their door. As I headed up to the house two ferocious guard dogs came charging out barking intently at me. Just kidding - they weren't ferocious. It was a Golden Retriever and a Sheltie and as soon as I said hello they wagged their tales and headed back to the house. So I went up and knocked on the door.

A really nice lady answered the door and I introduced myself, told her where we lived and the story about Sadie going missing. Her response was not what I expected. "I know you" she said. As I had no recollection of who she was and in the six years we lived at our place had never met my neighbors. I was a bit stunned. She went on to refresh my memory and put the pieces in place.

When we had first moved to our area I had to start my business from scratch. One of the things I had done was to go around to the various businesses in town to introduce myself. So way back ten years prior I had met a lady, Sally, that had mentioned she lived next to a really lovely horse farm – the people that owned it were great - and if I wanted to get involved with horses again that might be a place to start. Well – long story made short – eventually I called *the people that owned the really lovely horse farm*. I started riding one of their horses, we became best of friends and we bought our house and property from them.

We now live in one of the most superb places I could imagine. We have the pleasure and opportunity to use their seventy acre horse property for our horses and for walking Sadie through the miles and miles of trails. In other words without Sally our life would be very different right now. I think this was God's reminder that anyone you meet on any given day could be the one that changes your life – as Sally did for us ten years earlier.

Anyway, back to the search for Sadie. I had a nice chat with Sally and her husband. They had not spotted any stray dogs, but promised to keep a look out. Time had flown by and it was time now to head home and catch up with John. But, not before one more event to cap off the day. As I am walking back out the road from Sally's house and almost directly across from the little red barn I had seen earlier, there was another red barn with white "X's" on the doors. I don't know why I hadn't noticed it before. It was as if God was just putting an exclamation point on the day's happenings.

John was back at home after his efforts for the day as well. Besides all the searching we had done early in the morning and with the help of our friends Richard and Cathy, he had also gone out for a drive to look around. Still no Sadie. However, it felt good to come back home and have each other for love and support. I shared the remarkable events of my day. John also had a really important shift that afternoon. Up until today he had been functioning on hyper vigilance – dropping all his normal activities and thinking of nothing but finding Sadie. A person can only do that for so long before emotionally breaking.

Well again, God drops people in our lives for a reason. A friend had come with Richard and Cathy to help us search for the day. She had had dogs most of her life and has a pretty good idea of what makes them tick. As well, she was an independent party and not emotionally involved. In talking to John about where Sadie could possibly be and what she could possibly be up to and why in the heck if she was close by didn't she just come home – she made some comments that helped give John peace of mind.

Dogs are dogs she said. Their animal instinct makes them good at surviving in the wild and they do have a good sense of direction. From how John had described Sadie's personality to her she said Sadie is probably doing just fine and is out on an adventure and she will come back when she is either tired or hungry or just ready. Her saying that allowed John to take a deep breath – probably the first he had done in four days.

As it now was approaching about four in the afternoon and it was the time one of us would ordinarily be taking our girl out for a walk. We both agreed that, while we could have faith and believe she would be coming back home to us, one thing was certain. We really really missed having Sadie around. The house felt completely empty.

John and I went on one more walk together later in the evening and then called it a day.

Be on guard against the pit of self-pity. When you are weary or unwell, this demonic trap is the greatest danger you face. Don't even go near the edge of the pit. Its edges crumble easily, and before you know it, you are on the way down. It is much harder to get out of the pit than to keep a safe distance from it. That is why I tell you to be on guard.

There are several ways to protect yourself from self-pity. When you are occupied with praising and thanking Me, it is impossible to feel sorry for yourself. Also, the closer you live to Me, the more distance there is between you and the pit. Live in the Light of My Presence by fixing your eyes on Me. Then you will be able to run with endurance the race that is set before you, without stumbling or falling.

February 23rd
"Jesus Calling" – by Sarah Young

THE STORY
<u>DAY SIX</u>

It was now almost a week. John and I woke up somewhat numb in our very quiet house. A lot had happened over the previous few days. We were exhausted. We had looked everywhere we possibly could, put flyers out, contacted people and other than the Thursday evening not so much as a glimpse of our Sadie. The house felt empty. Now what???

God's answer to my Friday night prayer was playing in my head. "It will be Monday." This gave me a certain amount of peace and hope. I had to do all the activity the day before to satisfy my part that I had looked and searched – that is all I could humanly do. Even though it was only two and a half days from Friday night to Monday it seemed like an eternity. It was the hardest thing to just wait and trust.

So now it was Sunday and all I had to do was make it through this day. I felt inside – all right God, you have proven your point - sometimes you just want us to wait. So John and I did our best to try to get on with some other things that we had neglected all week and not focus only on our missing dog. However, we did take a couple walks out and around the neighborhood – just in case.

It was mostly an uneventful day. It actually gave us a chance to rest a little after the chaos and vigilance of the last several days.

The one thing of note to report - remember how early in this process I was questioning the use of intuitive or psychic information? Well, my scripture reading for this day – landing in my lap at just the time I needed it -'cause that is how God works - answered my question and cleared up my concern.

To paraphrase, in Acts 10 of the New Testament, Peter has a vision from God where he is instructed to do something that is forbidden by Jewish law. Peter was extremely perplexed, wherein, the response was – "If God says something is acceptable, don't say it isn't".

My conclusion for my situation is that God has a vision and a plan for each one of us. He will use whatever tools work and make sense to each individual to accomplish His purpose. I believe the intuitive information we utilized during this week highlighted His profound message – let go and trust God.

As the day drew to an end I felt kind of like a kid going to bed on Christmas Eve - the wonder, the anticipation, the hope. Would God really answer my prayer? Did I really hear his message saying it would be Monday? Or was I just coloring my thoughts with wishing and hoping?

Be still in the Light of My Presence, While I communicate Love to you. There is no force in the universe as powerful as My Love. You are constantly aware of limitations: your own and others'. But there is no limit to My Love; it fills all of space, time, and eternity.

Now you see through a glass, darkly, but someday you will see Me face to Face. Then you will be able to experience fully how wide and high and deep is My Love for you. If you were to experience that now, you would be overwhelmed to the point of feeling crushed. But you have an eternity ahead of you, absolutely guaranteed, during which you can enjoy My Presence in unrestricted ecstasy. For now, the knowledge of My loving Presence is sufficient to carry you through each day.

February 24th
"Jesus Calling" – by Sarah Young

THE STORY
<u>DAY SEVEN</u>

Today is the day!!! I'm off from work on Mondays so I would have the whole day to be prepared if/when Sadie came home. My first conversation with God on this beautiful day, besides the quick but sincere thank you for all the wonderful things in my life and I trust you Jesus, I trust you Jesus, was – "Okay it is Monday, what time today were you thinking of bringing Sadie back to us?"

I know God must have incredible patience and understanding with us and I think even a sense of humor. He knows our every thought, our every care, our every concern. On this occasion he was able to bear with my anxious impatience. I felt his gentle voice answer. "Be patient just a bit longer – it will be afternoon."

So John and I went on yet another walk together. It felt so weird without Sadie. We puttered around the house for a while. At about 11:00 am I gave a call to my good friend and neighbor that we bought our property from, Sue, to chat for a bit and to fill her in on the last few days and share that we still didn't have Sadie back.

I finished my call and it was getting closer to afternoon. I was doing my best to stay calm and be as "normal" as possible. Praying for the faith to believe that we would see Sadie by bedtime. I kept picturing it. I kept reassuring John we would have her back. We had a bit of lunch and then by around 1:00 pm we were both going stir crazy. This is the time Sadie would usually be following us around the house trying to make her point that it was time to go out on a walk.

My phone rang... John's phone number was on all the flyers and posters so we didn't really think a big deal. I looked at my caller ID and it was our friend Karen that I had talked to at the barn back on Thursday. Karen could be calling for any number of reasons – usually it is something to do with horses or the pony club – but, because of my head injury I hadn't been involved much. Hmmm I thought.

I answered the phone. "Hi Jennifer, **WE HAVE SADIE. She is OKAY.** She is in our car and we are on our way down to your house." My response was shock and disbelief. It is what I wanted to hear –but did I really just hear Karen say what I thought I heard? "We have Sadie. She is okay. She is in our car and we are on our way down to your house." I don't remember much else of what I said or of what she said other than - "We will be at your house with Sadie in a few minutes".

John was overhearing my conversation and as I got off the phone we both burst into joyous tears. Our Sadie was coming home!!!! As we put on our shoes and grabbed our jackets to go out to meet Karen our emotions were on hold....stunned. After almost a week of waiting, wondering, searching and hoping our prayers were answered – and, just as God had said it would. I must have said thank you Jesus ten thousand times in that five minutes we were waiting to see Karen drive in the driveway.

Finally, they arrived. They parked at the end of the barn because they had the horse trailer attached. Then seconds later we see our dear little girl, on a lead of course – just in case; but, tail wagging and healthy. By now both John and I had tears of happiness flooding down our face as we were reunited.

Sadie was OKAY. She was a little stinky and a little skinny – but there she was in the flesh right in front of us.

There are several miracles that came into play that day. The biggest one is that Karen and her teenage daughter, Emily, had planned to come down to the farm in the morning to ride horses in the arena. One of the rules of the farm is that if you want to come to the farm to ride you must first call to notify, Sue or Ken, the farm owners to let them know your plans – not just show up. Remember I said I had called Sue around 11:00 am to chat – well we were on the phone chatting at exactly the time Karen tried to call her. Sue and Ken do not have call waiting so Karen's call just went to the voicemail. It was almost 1:00 pm before Sue realized she had a message and called Karen back to say yes come on down.

I remember in several of my prayers saying - Lord, I know you have the power to put our Sadie down right in front of us. I know that wherever she is you can make it so she will either be found or come home. Karen and Emily live a mile southwest from us about a quarter mile off the main road and back up into the woods. The miracle that incredible

Monday afternoon was that at exactly the time they were driving out their driveway to come to our farm to ride - our Sadie was sitting in plain sight right on their road.

The other little miracles – Remember the information my intuitive friend Robin picked up back on Wednesday evening. Two important things – One, she had said Sadie would be found by a nice family with a teenager. Karen and Emily and family are the nicest family in the world and it was Emily, the teenager, that got out of the car - and Sadie, in her disoriented state, was willing to come up to her. The other interesting note from the information Robin had given is that in order to get from our house to where she was found it is highly likely that she did indeed go right past the little red barn that I had discovered on Saturday.

To this day I am still astounded at the powerful way God answered our prayers. He chose to put an exclamation point on the events of our week so that we would have no doubt that He had a hand in it. Our Sadie is back home safe and sound. I have no other choice than to believe **it was TRUE FAITH**.

Rest in My Presence, allowing Me to take charge of this day. Do not bolt into the day like a racehorse suddenly released. Instead, walk purposefully with Me, letting Me direct your course one step at a time. Thank Me for each blessing along the way; this brings Joy to both you and Me. A grateful heart protects you from negative thinking. Thankfulness enables you to see the abundance I shower upon you daily. Your prayers and petitions are winged into heaven's throne room when they are permeated with thanksgiving. In everything give thanks, for this is My will for you.

February 25th
"Jesus Calling" – by Sarah Young

EPILOGUE

It has been just over a year since these magical events touched my life. I am forever changed and challenged and reminded to trust God's plan for my life. It is when we quiet our mind and our spirit from the distractions of life that we hear His voice and His direction for our life. It is there that we find peace, joy, health and the answers to our prayers.

Sadie is still with us safe and sound and healthy - Maybe just a little more confident in herself having survived her venture off into the wild – kind of like a teenager who has gone off to college or spent some time traveling without their parents watching over their shoulder.

We have added some new fencing to our property - limiting and a little extra effort in some ways – but,

if it means keeping our girl safe and close to home
it is well worth the sacrifice.

I am still figuring out how to manage my life with
what might just be permanent changes in my brain.
I am finding success with just *being.* It means a lot
less activity than before. It means remembering to
schedule in time for rest and meditation – not such
a bad thing to do in this world that just seems to be
getting busier and faster. I have found that some
of the greatest gifts and joy come from pausing to
be grateful for what we have right in front of us.

**"This is the day the Lord has made,
we will rejoice and be glad in it" Psalms
118:24.**

PHOTO GALLERY

the farm

the view

the forest

the red barn

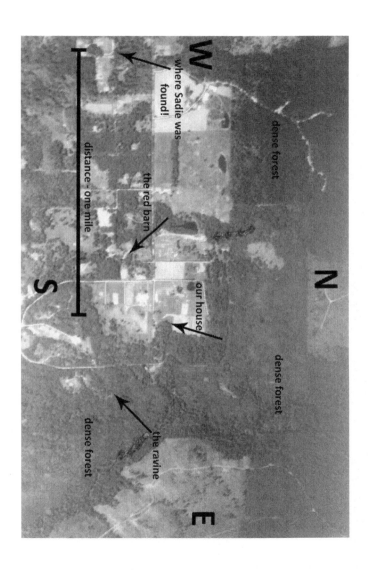

where Sadie was found!

the red barn

our house

the ravine

dense forest

dense forest

dense forest

distance - one mile

N

W

S

E

121

me and Sadie

Born and raised on a dairy farm in the beautiful Pacific Northwest, I developed a love of nature and animals. After spreading my wings and spending several years in the big city of Los Angeles, I returned to the Seattle area and settled on the Olympic Peninsula.

It was in this serene setting that I established my holistic medicine clinic to practice acupuncture. Working in my practice, I have had the pleasure of helping and caring for people for more than ten years. To compliment my work, I also reacquainted myself with riding and training two beautiful Thoroughbred horses on the farm we bought.

We acquired "Sadie" soon after and I was truly in animal heaven.

In Memory...

"True Faith"
2002 – 2014

Thank you TJ.